The
BLESSING

Giving the Gift *of* Unconditional Love and Acceptance

PARTICIPANT'S GUIDE

PARTICIPANT'S GUIDE

The
BLESSING

GIVING THE GIFT *of* UNCONDITIONAL
LOVE AND ACCEPTANCE

DVD SERIES FEATURING
JOHN TRENT, PH.D.

Based on the best-selling book The Blessing
by JOHN TRENT, Ph.D. and GARY SMALLEY

FOCUS
ON THE FAMILY

Colorado Springs, Colorado

CONTENTS

ACKNOWLEDGMENTS

There are so many people who have helped in launching The Blessing Challenge—and in putting together this small group series and workbook that share the core message of the biblical blessing. Most notably, we'd like to thank Bob Dubberley at Focus on the Family. He has been a tireless champion—and built a team of blessing champions at Focus—who are all committed to getting this message out to a new generation of parents, singles, couples, and grandparents. Special thanks goes to Larry Weeden and John Duckworth as well at Focus for their heroics in pulling together the Leader's and Participant's Guides.

We need to thank Debbie Wickwire at Thomas Nelson Publishers for her faithful prayers and for taking the lead in pulling the Nelson team around the message of the blessing—which started there at Nelson with the original book, *The Blessing*.

And finally, thanks to Hal Sandifer and his team at Red Giant Productions for their skill and going "all in" on making this series the best it can be. That includes the awesome work shooting the music videos that John Waller (www.johnwallermusic.com) and Shon Stewart (www.musicthat blessesothers.com) graced us with, adding their voices to The Blessing Challenge (www.TheBlessing.com).

—John Trent, Ph.D.

WELCOME!

What if there were a way you could improve your child's life—as well as the life of anyone else you care for—by doing something incredibly simple, yet amazingly powerful?

In God's Word we're shown and told about something called simply "the blessing." It springs off the pages of Scripture and begs to be practiced in our homes today. It is nothing short of a life-changing, life-giving gift that we can either choose to give our family and loved ones—or choose to withhold.

You'll find there's no middle ground. We are either, by our actions and words, adding to or taking away from our loved ones by the choice God sets before us. It's a choice that is nothing short of life or death, the blessing or the curse (Deuteronomy 30:19).

So get ready to learn about an amazingly practical, solidly biblical way to share unconditional love and acceptance with your family and others. Using five simple steps that add high value to your loved ones' lives today, you can clearly point them toward a positive future. It's a "you can do it" way to deepen your commitment to your family, friends, and church first—and to understand how and why God calls you to be a blessing to the rest of the world as well.

The DVD series you're about to watch will give you insights into this choice set before each of us. But it's in the discussion time sparked by this book that you'll really learn how to give and live the blessing. To help you do that, you'll find three steps in each chapter to guide you.

Log On: These are thoughts from Gary Smalley and me (we co-authored the original book, *The Blessing*) to help prepare you to get the most from the video you'll be viewing.

Screen Shots: Use this section as your guide in watching and discussing the DVD series.

Life App: Here you'll find suggestions that point you toward "bringing the blessing home"—actually giving the blessing to your family, your roommate, or others God has placed in your life story.

Even if you're not using this book as part of a small group, we urge you to take time to read and complete each chapter that links with the DVD.

And one last thing.

You'll hear a lot about The Blessing Challenge throughout the DVD series. The Blessing Challenge is a seven-year initiative of StrongFamilies.com, Focus on the Family, and Thomas Nelson Publishers, and involving many other ministries like Marriage Mentors, the Association of Marriage and Family Ministries, and the American Association of Christian Counselors. The goal: to see each of one million people choose to change the life of one child.

You do that by first learning how to bless others—which is what this DVD series is all about. Then we're asking you to go to www.TheBlessing.com and learn how to take an easy first step in giving the blessing to your family. Next, pick *one* child outside your home who will *not* receive the blessing unless you stand in the gap and give it to him or her.

That's how one million people are choosing to change the life of one child—by blessing their families and then reaching out to one person in need.

At www.TheBlessing.com you'll also find resources from StrongFamilies.com and Focus on the Family to help you go deeper, learn more, and discover how to create a culture of the blessing in your church and community. There's even an Institute for the Blessing, headed by Dr. Tony Wheeler, for those wanting coaching for their own family or church—and resources like Focus on the Family's *Thriving Family* magazine that can prove amazingly helpful in living the blessing each day.

We know you're way too busy to add one more challenge to your to-do list. But we also know that time spent learning about and bringing home the blessing will never be wasted. God bless you as you discover how to bless your family and that one child who's waiting for your blessing as well.

To see how singles, couples, and churches are jumping on board The Blessing Challenge, just visit us at www.TheBlessing.com.

—John Trent, Ph.D.
President, StrongFamilies.com and The Blessing Challenge

NEED HELP?

Many issues discussed in this series are difficult ones. Some people may need to address them in greater detail and depth. The DVD presentations and this guide are intended as general advice only, and not to replace clinical counseling, medical treatment, legal counsel, or pastoral guidance.

If you need more help, Focus on the Family maintains a referral network of Christian counselors. For information, call the Counseling Department at 1-855-771-4357. You can also find plenty of advice and encouragement at www.focusonthefamily.com.

ONE

It's YOUR CHOICE *to* BLESS

LOG ON
Preparing for the Video

Diane shook her head in disbelief. Her mind refused to accept what she'd heard. "Tell me exactly what my son said."

Her father-in-law replied, "We were talking about what day you'd return and how glad the two of you would be to see him. His little eyes looked down and he said, 'Dad will be glad to see me . . . but Mom won't. *She doesn't love me.*'"

Diane couldn't believe her eight-year-old son, Jerry, felt that way. If anything, she was afraid she loved him *too* much. She shared the problem with her husband, Don, and he suggested they read our book *The Blessing.*

Shortly after they'd gone through the book together, Diane went into her son's room to pray with him one night. She asked, "Honey, do you know what I really like about you?"

Without hesitation, Jerry said, *"Sure . . . nothing."*

Diane's heart sank.

Perhaps you're like Diane. You love your child or children dearly, but don't seem able to convince them you care. Perhaps it's your spouse or friend or parents who need your affirmation.

Perhaps you're like Jerry: Even as an adult, you honestly believe one or both of your parents don't, or didn't, love you. Maybe they were abusive, critical, had too-high expectations, or even abandoned you. It's possible that they, like Diane, simply didn't know how to express the love and acceptance necessary for you to feel loved and accepted.

Whether you've missed out on the blessing or need to learn to give it to those around you, this book and the DVD series it accompanies are tools for you to use to walk toward wholeness and positive relationships. The exercises are designed to help you learn and use the steps of the blessing, to provide the blessing to others, and to find the blessing for yourself.

Working through the process will take time, commitment, persistence, and perhaps some soul-searching. But if you master these principles, you'll find the effort well worthwhile. Diane did.

When her son, Jerry, admitted he couldn't think of anything about himself that she loved, Diane choked back tears. She said the first positive thing that popped into her mind: "Sweetheart, I do love the way you have such a good imagination and are able to make up such neat stories. I like that in your Daddy, too."

After that first night, Diane mentioned something she liked about Jerry every day. It became almost a ritual at bedtime. She reported, "Within months, he was sitting on my knee again and letting me kiss him goodnight. It was overwhelming to see him become a child again."

For nearly eight months, Diane had the joy of winning back her son's love and affection.

And then it happened—every mother's worst nightmare. While Jerry was delivering papers on his bicycle only a few blocks from their home, he was struck by a drunk driver and killed instantly.

In the midst of her grief, Diane brushed away tears and said, "I look back over those months preceding his death and thank God over and over that I was able to see my mistakes. God was gracious in giving me those special months. Jerry died knowing I loved him. I thank God for that."

SCREEN SHOTS
Watching and Discussing the DVD

After viewing the DVD's Session 1 segment, use questions like the following to help you think through what you saw and heard.

1. When it comes to giving the blessing, how are some people like broken gumball dispensers? If you've ever lost money in a vending machine or watched your purchase get stuck, how did you feel? How might a child or spouse feel if he or she were "this close" to getting the blessing but couldn't receive it?

2. Have you ever felt "this close" to blessing someone with an encouraging word or action, but couldn't seem to complete it? What kept you from following through?

3. If you were in that living room with Dr. John Trent, what question would you most want to ask him about the blessing? Would you want to ask him out loud in front of the group, or get him an anonymous note? Why?

4. Look up Deuteronomy 30:19. If "life" means stepping toward others and "death" means stepping away, which do you think most people choose in their relationships? How might you "choose life" in the following situations?

- Your eight-year-old son wants an elaborate pirate theme at his birthday party, and you just want to get it over with.
- Your 21-year-old daughter, only six months from college graduation, announces that she's quitting school and moving to Nashville to try to make it as a country singer.
- Your spouse is depressed after 18 months of unsuccessfully looking for a job, and you can't stand the stress and joylessness in your home anymore.
- Your father, a widower who never had a kind word for you when you were growing up, wants you to stay in his house for six weeks—taking care of him as he recovers from hip replacement surgery.
- Your 12-year-old stepdaughter refuses to obey your limits on TV watching because "you're not my real mom."

5. John Trent says that God never tires of blessing us. Why might a parent get tired of blessing a child, or vice versa? Why might a spouse get tired of blessing his or her mate?

6. In which of the following situations is blessing like bowing the knee, dipping a flag, or adding value or weight on a scale?
- You put a "My Child Is an Honor Student" bumper sticker on your car.
- You sing "How Great Thou Art" in church.
- You ask your child to show you how to use an app on your smartphone.
- You take a photo of your mother standing in front of the flower garden she's worked so hard to nurture.

7. Do you think more people "curse" others by swearing at them or by failing to bless them? Why? Which do you think is worse? Why?

8. If failing to bless others is like damming up a stream of life-giving water, which of the following is most like the "climate" in which you grew up? Which is most like your current household? What climate do you forecast you'll be living in five years from now?
   - desert
   - semi-arid
   - temperate
   - rain forest
   - other _____

9. Read John 4:4-26. How did Jesus bless the woman at the well? How might someone else have "cursed" the woman? What would you have done? Why?

10. John Trent will have more to say about "reversing the curse" in future sessions. At this point, on a scale of 1 to 10 (10 highest), what do you think the chances would be of "reversing the curse" in the following cases? Why?
    - You grew up in a home that was an emotional desert, and want things to be different for your spouse and children.
    - You're trying to encourage your kids more than your parents encouraged you, but your spouse thinks you're overdoing it and making your children self-centered.
    - You'd like to forgive your mother for ignoring the way your cousin abused you as a child, but your mother passed away three years ago.

11. Look at Genesis 27:34, 38, in which Esau begs his father for a blessing. Do most people in our culture do that? If so, are their requests ignored? If not, how can you tell when someone needs a blessing?

12. How did you feel when you heard John Waller's song? Do you know anyone who might be especially blessed by hearing this song this week? If you had to convey its message to that person in three words, what would they be?

LIFE APP
Applying What You've Learned

Besides strengthening or rebuilding family relationships and producing a sense of self-worth in children, the blessing also helps ensure closer, happier social ties with others as children grow up.

In a 36-year study reported several years ago in the *Journal of Personality and Social Psychology*, psychologists Carol Franz, David C. McClelland, and Joel Weinberg found that children who receive physical affection and warmth are apt to have closer marriages and friendships, better mental health, and greater work success. Affection from Dad is as influential and lasting as affection from Mom, according to the study. But warm affection from both parents is most likely to result in a well-adjusted adult with a strong sense of internal security.

That same study showed the opposite to be true of children who didn't receive warmth and affection from their parents. These children will more likely lack personal acceptance, which in turn leads to difficulty in making decisions and relating well to people.

Without the blessing, some people carry a huge reservoir of unreleased anger that eventually explodes and spreads hurt over everyone around. Others are bound by a paralyzing fear that keeps them from functioning at their full capacity—fear of what people think, fear of failure, fear of rejection, fear of not measuring up, fear of fear itself.

People who've never heard affirming words or who were never encouraged often lack communication skills—damaging their careers and relationships. Pessimism, another result of missing the blessing, can actually shorten one's life span.

Everyone needs to receive the blessing.

Rachel didn't. Now in her mid-50s, Rachel will not invite friends for coffee or lunch. Her self-esteem is so low that she'd rather be lonely than risk their saying no and thus feeling rejected.

While she was growing up, Rachel believed her mother favored her younger brother. Instead of affirming Rachel's value, her mother taught her to stay in the background and consider everyone else better and more important. Rachel never felt cherished. As a result, she failed to find the blessing, and her sense of inferiority became so strong that no amount of affirmation has been able to change her negative self-perception.

How about you? Were you "blessed" during your early years? How does that affect you today?

To get started in answering these questions, try describing your family when you were six or eight years old. Think back to a typical mealtime. Who was there? What was the conversation about? What was the atmosphere (happy, at odds, silent)?

Now look at individual family members.

Do you feel that your father generally approved or disapproved of you? What did he like about you? What did he dislike?

How did he show approval or disapproval?

How did you feel about your father when you were a child? When you were a teen? As an adult?

Did your mother generally approve or disapprove of you? What did she like about you? What did she dislike?

How did she show approval or disapproval?

How did you feel about your mother when you were a child? When you were a teen? As an adult?

Describe the relationship you had with your brothers and sisters when you were a child.

What is your current relationship with your siblings?

Record briefly how other significant people, if any, affected your life.

How do you see yourself today? Are you successful? A failure? Happy? Depressed? Yearning? All "together" emotionally?

To help understand your current relationships, examine your family groupings as you were growing up. The space below represents the whole of your universe. Draw a stick figure in the center to stand for you; write your name on it. Draw and name the other members of your family as they related to you in your earliest memories of family life.

Did Dad dominate? If so, make him a little bigger and put him at the top. If Mom was submissive, but you felt she was in close relationship to Dad, draw her somewhat smaller, a little lower, but close to Dad. Was Mom the driving force? Put her higher. Were Mom and Dad repressed? Affectionate? Touching? Far away?

Were certain family members always close, bonded together? Connect them with a solid line. Were there family members who were sometimes close and sometimes distant? Connect them with a broken line.

If one of the children acted as part-time or substitute parent, draw a circle around him or her and write how you felt about him or her.

If your family grouping changed drastically (due to a move, loss of job, birth, adoption, divorce, remarriage, or death) when you were growing up, draw another universe and show the new relationships.

Would you say that you "received your parents' blessing" as a child? Why or why not?

Do you feel you have that blessing now?

If you feel neither of your parents blessed you, how would you have liked them to behave?

That's plenty to think about for now. Considering your upbringing will provide a good foundation for the rest of this series.

Completing the exercises in this book also will help you give your children, spouse, friends, and others the advantages of the blessing. Like Diane, you may want to praise God for what you learn as relationships with your family and friends grow.

As you begin your journey toward the blessing, we want to give you *our* blessing. Without knowing who you are, we know you are special in God's eyes. He cares for you, and we care too. We know that, if you diligently give yourself to learning and practicing the steps in this book, you'll become a person of blessing.

In a later chapter we'll look at how the presence or absence of the blessing affects our relationships. Next, though, we'll take a close look at the blessing itself.

TWO

The POWER
of YOUR TOUCH

LOG ON
Preparing for the Video

What is this "blessing," this important act that no one can live well without?

Here's one way to explain it: "words and actions that provide an indelible picture of affirmation in a person's mind and memory." To bless is to honor, praise, salute. To be blessed is to be given power for success, prosperity, and longevity.

We can give our children, spouse, parents, or friends the benefits of daily blessing. It doesn't have to be a big production; it can be something simple. How often have you done the following things?

- really listened when others talk
- let a child spend a day with you at work
- admitted you make mistakes
- left a plate of cookies with an "I love you" note
- used any one of hundreds of other ways of saying, "You're special; I care"

Parents can bless children, spouse can bless spouse, friend can bless friend, child can bless parent, church workers can bless church members. It only takes a knowledge of how to do it, the desire, and a commitment to express love and caring.

In our book *The Blessing,* we explored five elements necessary to giving a blessing, as given in the Old Testament. These five elements, or steps, were

- giving meaningful touch
- speaking words of blessing
- expressing high value
- picturing a special future
- making an active commitment to seeing the blessing come to pass

To get acquainted, let's take a brief look at each of these steps in the DVD segment.

SCREEN SHOTS
Watching and Discussing the DVD

After viewing the DVD's Session 2 segment, use questions like the following to help you think through what you saw and heard.

1. Dr. John Trent names five elements that make up blessings in the Bible. Which one would be easiest for you to give? Why? What can you do about the rest?

2. The first element of the blessing is appropriate, meaningful touch. Which of the following would be appropriate but not meaningful? Meaningful but not appropriate? Both? Neither?
    - offering your wife a "fist bump" after teasing her about being overweight

- punching your eight-year-old son, who has just brought home a good report card, in the shoulder—hard enough that he says, "Ow!"
- briefly hugging your 17-year-old daughter in front of other students before leaving her at college
- holding your husband's hand during his father's funeral

3. The second element is spoken words. How would the impact of the following be different if they didn't involve spoken words?
   - a wedding ceremony
   - awarding diplomas at high school graduation
   - a baptism
   - presenting the cake at a birthday party

   How would you convince someone who "isn't a talker" to speak up in order to bless a child or spouse?

4. The third element is attaching high value. How did Jesus do that in the following passages? How has a teacher, coach, or relative done that for you?
   - Luke 12:6-7
   - Mark 14:3-9
   - Matthew 19:13-15
   - John 13:1-5

5. The fourth element is a special future. How would you change the following "dire predictions" into "special futures"?
   - "If you don't quit daydreaming, you're going to flunk out."
   - "You think you're funny, but one of these days somebody's going to get mad at your 'jokes' and punch you in the nose."
   - "If you don't take some risks, you'll never make any money."

6. The fifth element is active commitment. Which of the following are you willing to commit to right now? Which might you commit to when the series is done? Which do you think you'll never commit to?
    - finishing this DVD series
    - personally blessing two million people
    - blessing your child or spouse in the next 24 hours
    - finding someone outside your family who hasn't received the blessing and giving that to him or her
    - other _____

7. John Trent describes his mother as "a world-class person of blessing." Can you think of anyone who might describe you that way? If not, which of the following titles might fit you best?
    - Blesser of the County
    - the Anti-Blesser
    - a Minor League Person of Blessing
    - other _____

8. How did John's mentor, Doug Barram, use meaningful, appropriate touch when blessing others? If you're a parent, what kind of touch has your child appreciated most? How has that changed over time?

9. Which of the following is most like your experience with appropriate, meaningful touch?
    - the Trent boys' reluctance to be seen hugging their mom
    - the congregation that lays hands on its kids during the service
    - the husband whose greatest need was physical touch because he didn't have it as a child
    - other _____

10. Read about the blessings Isaac gave his sons in Genesis 27. Is there a practice in our culture that accomplishes the same thing as this kind of blessing? Do you think our society would be better off if this type of blessing were part of our tradition? Why or why not?

11. If you had to add a sixth element to make the blessing even more powerful, what would it be?

12. If you could travel back in time to visit yourself at age 12, on your wedding day (if you're married), and at the birth of your first child (if you have any), who would you bless and how would you do it?

LIFE APP
Applying What You've Learned

Element 1: Appropriate, Meaningful Touch

Before even a word is spoken, the blessing is conveyed by touch.

One five-year-old loved the way her mother tousled the girl's hair when walking by. "It makes me feel special," she told her mom.

Touch played a part in biblical examples of blessing. In Genesis 48, Jacob blessed Ephraim and Manasseh by putting his hands on their heads. The act of touch communicates warmth and affirmation.

Touch also conveys acceptance. A hand on the shoulder, an arm curled round in a hug, a kiss, can say, "You're all right. I care."

Max found this out when he was 45 and near death after a major heart attack. He'd grown up knowing his dad loved him—not from anything that was said, only by the look in his dad's eyes. His father, a German farmer, was raised in such a way that he could never bring himself to say "I love you" or otherwise verbalize his affection.

When Max was an adult, he left the farm and moved to California, where he was when he had the heart attack. Warned that Max might not survive, his wife called the family.

Max's dad flew all the way across the country to be with his son. When he arrived, he came to his son's room in the ICU where he was hooked up to various tubes and monitoring equipment.

Max told us on the radio that he had never, even once, heard his father verbally tell him, "I love you." He knew his father loved him, but he'd always longed to hear those words of blessing.

"But that day," Max told us, "my father did something where I know now for a fact that I did get his blessing."

"What was that?" we asked, our interest sky-high.

"He simply pulled up a chair and sat next to me . . . and held my hand for about an hour."

We were both touched by his story, but that's when he dropped the bombshell. "And if you think that's something," Max continued, "let me tell you the rest of the story. Three days after my father flew cross-country to be at my bedside, *he died.*

"Today, I thank God for my heart attack, because if it had never happened, I wouldn't have known for a fact that I had my father's blessing like I know now."

How has a touch shown you love, lifted your spirits, made you feel better, encouraged you, or added a sparkle to your day?

Ask your child, spouse, or friend to answer the above question. Do you have a role in that story?

Researchers describe meaningful touch as a gentle touch, stroke, kiss, or hug given by significant people in our lives. Touch becomes meaningful when the one touching desires to bless the one touched and reaches out for the other person's benefit, not his or her own.

Meaningful touch is appropriate touch. You can hug your own children, but not every child on the block or in the Sunday school. Even if your intent is to bless, the touch must fit your relationship with that person.

In today's society, with abuse—particularly sexual abuse—so rampant, we need to limit touch to what is meaningful but appropriate. You can give a child a pat on the shoulder. You can spontaneously hug a friend or clasp hands with an acquaintance. Some people are comfortable with a close hug, while others prefer to maintain space around themselves.

What meaningful touch are you comfortable or uncomfortable receiving? (Example: *I hate being patted on the top of my head, but a hand on my arm is welcome.*)

Above all, touch symbolizes acceptance. Read the account of Jesus healing the leper in Mark 1:40-42. What was the first thing Jesus did?

What does a willingness to shake your hand, to put an arm around your shoulder, or to reach out and draw you close say to you?

How do you feel if someone refuses to shake hands or touch you?

Neglecting to meaningfully touch our children starves them of genuine acceptance—so much so that it can drive them into the arms of someone who is all too willing to touch them. Yet another study showed that it takes eight to ten meaningful touches each day to maintain emotional and physical health.

The need for meaningful touch doesn't disappear when we become teenagers and young adults. Often through these years we may say we don't want to be touched, but deep down we long for meaningful touch from our parents.

When my (Gary's) son Greg and I were on a talk show together, the interviewer asked Greg for an example of something I had done that Greg really appreciated.

Greg answered, "When I was in junior high, I used to say, 'Dad, I don't want to talk about it, and don't hug me.' Well, I'm glad now that my dad didn't listen to me. What I was really saying was, 'Dad, I do want you to listen to me and I do need you to hug me.' Dad was great. He did the right thing."

That doesn't mean, of course, that every child is ready to be touched. Alice almost couldn't stand her preschool son because he looked so much like his father, who'd deserted her before Tommy was born. To Alice, little Tommy represented the biggest mistake of her life, and her rage at Tommy's father fell on the boy. The only time she touched Tommy was in anger.

While studying *The Blessing* in a single parents' class at our church, Alice was confronted with the reality of how she treated her son. She decided to start hugging Tommy.

At home that evening, she held out her arms and said, "Come, Tommy. Mommy wants to hug you."

Tommy ran in the opposite direction. His experience was that when Mom reached for him, it was in anger.

Alice didn't give up. She chased him around the house until she finally corralled him and gave him a hug. For over three months she persisted in giving Tommy meaningful touch, standing by the door each morning and hugging him before he went out to play.

Finally Tommy realized that the hugs were there to stay. One day Alice held out her arms to him from across the room, and he ran into them. For the first time he hugged her and she could hug him back.

Little Tommy was afraid of the outstretched hands because they'd dealt blows, not hugs, in the past. Others shy away from touch because physical closeness makes them uncomfortable.

Do you identify with Alice? With Tommy?

How comfortable do you think your children are with your touch?

Why do they feel this way?

If your children are growing up in a home where touching isn't done, hugs are nonexistent, and physical closeness is taboo, they'll feel uncomfortable when people get too close even though they'll earnestly desire that closeness.

Begin with safe touch. Which of these non-threatening touches have you used?

- touching the elbow
- a ten-second back rub
- patting a shoulder
- smoothing a hand over your child's hair
- giving a high-five

Element 2: Spoken Words

Touch, however important, can't carry the whole load. A verbal message of acceptance, appreciation, or encouragement is the next step in giving the blessing.

When Jacob blessed Manasseh and Ephraim, he not only laid his hands on their heads, he also said, "In your name will Israel pronounce this blessing: 'May God make you like Ephraim and Manasseh'" (Genesis 48:20).

With words we can express acceptance and love, both vital to emotional health and well-being. Or we can express rejection and degradation.

Denise grew up in a home where her father saw to it that she received every element of the blessing. He encouraged her, went to her sports activities and school open houses, and supported her every way he could.

One of Denise's best memories was her father's pet name for her: "Angel Darling." He even made up a little song that used her pet name and told of his love. The last time she heard the song was just before her father died. He asked her to sit on the edge of his bed, gave her a hug, and sang the song to his "little girl."

Denise said, "It was hurtful and healing at the same time. I hurt because I knew it was the last time I'd ever hear him sing my song, but it meant so much to me. It was Dad's way of saying, 'You're special and I've always loved you.' "

Donna grew up in just the opposite kind of home. Her father provided one of the most degrading homes imaginable. Donna was tall and slender, stunningly attractive, but when I (John) met her she refused to dress in any color but black. In part, her color choice came from the darkness she carried inside from hearing the nickname her father called her each day: "Demon Daughter." Donna lived a miserable life until she met Christ and He freed her from the title her father had bestowed.

Think back to your growing years and the words people said to you. What words of acceptance or encouragement do you remember? What effect did they have on you?

Did you hear words of degradation, as Donna did? If so, give an example.

What words of encouragement or discouragement do you say to those you should bless?

What effect do you think your words have on those people?

Element 3: Expressing High Value

To be effective, our words and actions must express our esteem for the one we're blessing and affirm that this person is valuable. In the Scriptures, recognition is based on who a person is, not on his or her performance.

In Jacob's blessing of Ephraim and Manasseh, he said, "May they be called by my name and the names of my fathers Abraham and Isaac . . ." (Genesis 48:16). Their value lay not in anything they had done, but in who they were— sons of his son, now to be reckoned as his sons to receive the blessing God gave to Abraham.

We can say or do a wide variety of things to attach high value to another person. To which of the following acts do you attach high value?

___ Praising thoughtfulness

___ Acknowledging good qualities or character traits

___ Rewarding good performance

___ A pat on the shoulder for an obedient attitude

___ A note in the lunch bag saying, "You're tops."

Which one of the acts above is based on what someone does rather than who he or she is?

How do you suppose these words make a person feel?

Another way to express high value is by our presence, as Alex discovered. I (John) met Alex on a plane recently, and we fell into conversation. When Alex learned that I worked with families, he asked for advice. His son was a leading player in Little League in terms of home runs and extra base hits—a good member of the team, but a goof-off in the dugout.

The father said, "Tell me if I did something wrong. My wife thinks I did. She's really upset with me."

"What happened?"

"We were at the game, and Joe, my son, was messing around, so I pulled him over and said, 'Listen. Either you get serious, in the dugout as well as on the ball field, or I'm leaving.'"

His son shaped up for a while, but soon began to clown around again. Sure enough, the father yelled at his son and stormed out—missing the rest of the boy's big playoff game, including his game-losing strikeout in the last inning.

That father told me, "I think I did what he deserved. But my wife is sure I did the wrong thing. What's your opinion?"

Instead of responding, I asked, "Did your dad ever do something like that to you?"

Instantly, Alex hung his head. "All the time. My dad used to motivate me by his absence. He withdrew himself to punish me. He still does. If he comes to visit and I do something that displeases him, he'll up and leave." His father, who could attach high value to his son with his presence, chose not to.

It was obvious that this man was carrying a negative pattern from one generation to the next. He not only missed the game, he missed an opportunity to comfort his son and say, "I love you anyway. It's OK. I'm still proud of you." He could have reversed a negative pattern and attached value to his son with his presence and a few words: "I'm staying because you're important to me."

How did a significant person in your life let you know he or she valued you highly?

Give an example of how you show your children, spouse, family, or friends that you value them.

Element 4: Picturing a Special Future

Well-meaning but ill-informed parents try to motivate their children with negative statements. Too many children hear, "If you don't [whatever], you'll never amount to anything," or "Hey, Dum-dum, what went wrong this time?"

Instead, we can give those we bless a sense of security and confidence by conveying that the gifts and character traits they have right now are attributes God can bless and use in the future.

If we look back at our example with Jacob blessing Manasseh and Ephraim, we see that he pictured a marvelous future: They would be held up as examples of being blessed by God. He also included God's blessing of their becoming great nations.

A message about one's future can be given without words, as in the case of Mike and Doug. Mike had musical talent and had made all-state choir. On the afternoon of Mike's performance of the year, his brother Doug had a soccer practice. Not a game, just a routine practice.

Mike's dad, who had been a pro athlete, chose to go to the soccer practice rather than the choir presentation. His decision told Mike, "What you're interested in, what you want to be, the talent you have, who you are isn't important to me."

Mike struggled all his life to feel accepted by others because of this incident and many more indications that music wasn't as important as sports. He could never feel that what he accomplished had any merit.

Did you have a similar experience? How did it make you feel? What has been the long-term effect on your life?

Did your parents or other significant persons do or say anything to assure you of your capability to have a bright future?

In what ways, if any, are you copying your parents as you bless or withhold the blessing from others?

Element 5: An Active Commitment

This element is a "kicker." It requires sticking with the program even when your child misbehaves or the person you're blessing disappoints you and you're ready to toss up your hands in despair. It's committing time and energy to involvement in that person's life to see that the words of blessing you speak come to pass.

Words alone, even words of high value picturing a special future combined with touch, cannot completely communicate the blessing. A commitment to carry out the blessing is essential. Everyone intent on giving the blessing needs to rely on the Lord to provide strength and staying power to confirm a child's, spouse's, or friend's blessing.

Jane was a young adult who missed the blessing. As a result, she'd become so shattered she couldn't relate to anyone. She withdrew emotionally until her parents were unable to deal with her. Finally, she was taken into a home for treatment. Stan and Amy, new Christians, were chosen to work with Jane. They determined to visit her and tell her of their love and of Jesus' love for her.

The first day, they entered her room and said hello. Jane looked at them through lackluster eyes, picked up her chair, turned it to face the wall, and sat down with her back to them.

Stan and Amy looked at each other and drew a quick breath of prayer. Amy said, "We just came to tell you we love you. If there's anything we can do for you, we want to do it."

Stan echoed, "Yes. We love you. We want to help you."

The next day, they returned. Again Jane picked up her chair, turned it toward the wall, and sat down. Again Stan and Amy told her they loved her and added that Jesus loved her, too. The next day was the same, and the next, and the next.

In fact, daily for months, Stan and Amy kept their commitment to bless Jane. Jane sat facing the wall. When they tried to touch her shoulder, she huddled into herself and ducked her head. Despite discouragement, Stan and Amy kept their commitment and went on visiting Jane.

Finally, one day *almost a year* from the first time they saw her, they entered the room. Jane looked at them, nodded briefly, and sat facing them.

Feeling as if they'd achieved a major victory, Stan and Amy told her again of their love and Jesus' love. It wasn't long until Jane was talking and even letting them hug her when they left.

In what ways can you remember your parents, spouse, or another significant person actively working as Stan and Amy did to see that you got their blessing?

Even if you can't recall that kind of experience, can you think of anyone in your current circle who could benefit from your genuine commitment to bless him or her? What first step might you take to do that?

THREE

The MOST VALUABLE WORDS *You'll* EVER SAY

LOG ON
Preparing for the Video

Meaningful touch can be more powerful than words. But without the right words, the blessing circuit is never closed and the message of the blessing doesn't get through.

The power of words comes from God. In the beginning, He spoke and all creation came into being. From the time He walked with Adam and Eve in the garden to the commandments to the prophets to the ministry of Christ, to the Scriptures, God has used words to bless, discipline, teach, and more.

His words are always effective. "So is my word that goes out from my mouth: It will not return to me empty, but will accomplish what I desire and achieve the purpose for which I sent it" (Isaiah 55:11).

Our words also have an effect. They may not always do what we intend, but they're mighty in affecting the lives of those we speak to.

Positive words bless; negative words demolish. Silence can destroy someone who looks to us for a blessing. Both people and relationships suffer in the absence of spoken words of love, encouragement, and support—words of blessing.

Unless a person hears something like, "I love you; you're special," he or she will never feel completely blessed. Though a parent may shower gifts and material goods on a child and do many other things in the child's best interest, that child will experience a void that results in incredible heartache and hurt unless the parent's actions are accompanied by accepting, acknowledging words.

Children desperately need to hear a spoken blessing from their parents; husbands and wives need to hear words of love and acceptance on a regular basis from their spouses. Friends need to hear the blessing from friends; parents need to hear it from children.

One word of praise or blessing can last a lifetime. I (John) had a good athletic career during high school, but one coach I had praised me only once in four years. I still remember the play. I remember being called to the sidelines. I remember what he was wearing and the hat he had on. He pulled me out for one play to praise me, and for me it made four years' worth of effort worthwhile.

In addition to spoken words, biblical blessing involves attaching high value.

By deliberate decision, we attach value to family, neighbors, and people in our church or our workplace. We must value all those whom God puts into our lives and treat them with respect. However, God gives us certain people who need more of our time and energy. For them, we have to plan more specific, in-depth ways to show we value them.

Attaching high value isn't always easy. The people we need to honor may seem unworthy of our esteem—a mother who deserted us, a child who disobeys and dishonors us, a father who abused us. If judged by performance, these people may not rate higher than a "1.3" on the 1 to 10 scale. Regardless of how these family members treat us, we need to honor them—to respond not by how we feel but according to God's command.

Attaching high value is based on who a person is, not on what he or she does. We must determine to value others just as parents love their children—unconditionally, regardless of what they do.

SCREEN SHOTS
Watching and Discussing the DVD

After viewing the DVD's Session 3 segment, use questions like the following to help you think through what you saw and heard.

1. Would you bless your child or spouse by comparing his or her smell to that of a field (Genesis 27:27)? Why or why not? What are three modern comparisons you could use instead? To get you started, here are some examples:
   - "You're so smart, people would line up like they do at Disney World to get your advice."
   - "Your eyes are as blue as the startup screen on my laptop."
   - "If I saw you on eBay, I wouldn't just bid—I'd 'Buy It Now.'"

2. Why do you think God the Father blessed God the Son with spoken words (Matthew 3:17; 17:5)? Wouldn't Jesus "just know" His Father approved of Him? What does this tell you about the need to bless others with spoken words?

3. One father of three girls used "daddy-daughter dates" to bless his kids verbally. What kind of "date" might you plan for blessing the following family members?

- a five-year-old son who likes dinosaurs
- a wife who gained three pounds on Weight Watchers last week
- a 16-year-old daughter who just had a fight with her boyfriend
- a husband who loves hiking

4. Why do you think Jesus attached high value to "rejects" like lepers, tax collectors, and poor people? What might He see in your child, spouse, or neighbor that you've been missing?

5. Which two of the following awards would mean the most to you? Why?
   - an Oscar
   - a "World's Greatest Grandparent" coffee mug from your grandson
   - a Super Bowl ring
   - a homemade card from your daughter that says, "I love you"
   - a Nobel Prize for literature
   - an "Excellent" sticker on your essay from your favorite grade-school teacher

   What impromptu award could you give your child or spouse today?

6. A father's blessing at his son's pastoral ordination service helped sustain the son through half a century of ministry. If you added up all the verbal blessings you've given your child so far, how long do you think they'd keep him or her going? If you added up all those you've given your spouse so far, how long do you think they'd last him or her?

7. If you had to affirm your child with words, but without mentioning any of his or her talents or achievements, how would you do it? Why might it be important to do that?

8. Do you think you'd be watching this DVD series today if John Trent's father had given John the blessing? Do you think you'd be watching it if your own parents had done a better job of blessing you? Why or why not?

9. Why does John Trent still carry around an old letter from his great-uncle? What message to you, whether it's on paper or in your memory, means that much to you? What message *from* you might mean that much to someone else?

10. Do you agree that the blessing is a choice? Why or why not? Which three of the following have had the most influence on your blessing choices so far?
    - time
    - money
    - your parents
    - your personality
    - the Bible
    - your child's or spouse's behavior
    - other _____

11. When you hear stories about how powerfully the blessing—or lack of it—can shape a person's life, what's your reaction?
    - "This is too much responsibility."
    - "Blessings are overrated."
    - "I've got to start right now."

- "I'm not blessing until somebody blesses me."
- other _____

12. If you needed to tell your child that you value him or her highly, which two of the following ways would you prefer to use? Why? What if you were communicating the same message to your spouse?
    - e-mail
    - face-to-face talk
    - snail-mail letter
    - greeting card
    - newspaper ad
    - Facebook page
    - texting
    - phone call
    - other _____

LIFE APP
Applying What You've Learned

How have words affected your life? Think back to a time when you felt blessed or cursed. What was said? What were the immediate and long-term results?

If answering these questions reopened old wounds, what do you think it will take to heal them?

If a parent gives a child meaningful touch and says the right words, the child feels blessed. If a parent gives a child meaningful touch but says the wrong words or no words, the child feels a void and will always search for the blessing. The same is true of spouses or friends.

Why? Because words have incredible power to build us up or tear us down emotionally.

This power can be misused, sometimes with tragic results. The destructive power of fiery words or cold silence can affect us for the rest of our lives. Negative words can come from parents who don't care about their children or from parents or spouses who missed the blessing themselves and don't know how to pass it on. Most of the time, negative words are spoken by loving parents without thought to the consequences.

Demeaning words make a person feel less intelligent, less capable, less worthy, less loved, less lovely, less wanted, less of a person. These words destroy.

For each of the demeaning phrases below, imagine a scene where they might be said. Write some words of blessing that would encourage instead of demean. Here's an example:

"Clumsy idiot!" (Someone may have tripped over something or knocked a glass full of milk over on the table. Words of blessing: "That's okay, Bobby. Everyone has accidents from time to time. When I was your age I did the same thing.")

"Why try? You can't do it."

"Messed up again, didn't you?"

"Can't you do anything right?"

People who hear demeaning words tend to believe them after a time, and almost always live down to them.

Harsh words are spoken in anger; they're words of abuse. That was the case in the Wilson family. Neither Dad nor George, the oldest son, spoke under a roar. Whenever a family member did something irritating, the whole neighborhood heard about it.

Harsh words hurt. For the rest of their lives, children may stumble over the hurtful words spoken to them. What are some harsh words you remember?

What blessing words would have been more effective in the situation?

Empty words are another problem. Some children hear words of blessing, but there is no follow-up. Promises aren't kept, actions don't fit the words, or lack of meaningful touch denies the message. The words lose all meaning, and the child is left unfulfilled. He or she learns distrust.

Which, if any, of these kinds of incidents happened to you?

____ "Let's go swimming after dinner tonight. It'll be a treat for the whole family." Then, when the dishes are done, you hear, "No, not tonight. Dad's tired. We'll do it next week."

____ "She's my little jewel. I don't know what I'd do without her." But as soon as the company leaves, you hear, "Go do something. What are you hanging around for?"

____ "Of course I love you. You're my child [or wife/husband], aren't you?"

____ "Look, Daddy, see my new haircut!" Dad says it's really neat, but never looks up from the paper.

What common message do these vignettes convey?

What about an *absence of words*? In many homes today, both parents are working overtime, and a "family night" makes an appearance about as often as Halley's comet. Life is so hectic that, for many parents, that "just right" time to communicate a spoken blessing never quite comes around.

"Oh, it's not that big a deal," some parents say. "They know I love them and that they're special without my having to say it." Quite the contrary; to children, silence has communicated something far different from love and acceptance.

Some parents feel love, but keep it hidden so deep inside it doesn't have a chance to surface.

Sometimes words aren't spoken because there are family rules about what you talk about and what you don't.

In one family, no conversation was allowed to get deep enough to touch real emotions. You didn't talk about things that might make you cry or even feel. The unspoken rule was so deeply ingrained that Ellen, one of the daughters, felt an insurmountable barrier when it came to conversation with her mother. Now in her mid-50s, Ellen is taking care of her mother, who is dying of cancer. The taboo still holds. They don't talk about what hurts most, what is heaviest on their hearts.

Absence of words causes suffering. Unmet needs for security and acceptance act like sulfuric acid and eat away at relationships between parent and child, between spouses, between friends. The relationships disintegrate.

Perhaps most destructive is the parent who is always home, but never says words of acceptance. This parent sends a double message: "I'm always here, but you can never come to me." Such people put a vast emotional distance between themselves and their children.

If you were given the "silent treatment" as a child, why do you think your parents withheld words of blessing?

How well are you able to express your feelings to others?

Over the course of your life, which of the following do you feel your parents gave you?

____ More words of blessing

____ More demeaning, harsh, empty words

____ More silence

How do you think your parents really felt about you?

Are you repeating the same word usage as your parents?

So why do we wait to give a spoken message of blessing? Why do we keep putting it off? Why do you?

Are you angry with the person you might bless? Are you too busy? Has it been so long, you'd feel embarrassed?

Most procrastination is caused by fear. We might fear the reaction our words will provoke: rejection, amazement, doubt, laughter, or misunderstanding. We might fear that we won't seem macho if we say something sentimental. Some parents think they may "inflate their child's ego."

Here are other reasons people give for not blessing others. Mark any you've felt.

_____ "I'm afraid if I praise them, they'll take advantage of me and won't do what I say."

_____ "Communication is too much like work. I can't work all day, then work all night talking to my wife."

_____ "I just don't know what to say."

_____ "They know I love them without my having to say it."

_____ "If I get started, I'll have to make a habit of it."

_____ "Telling children their good points is like putting on perfume. A little is okay, but put on too much and it stinks."

_____ "My parents never gave me the blessing; I don't know how."

None of these are valid reasons for withholding words of blessing. The benefits of blessing others far outweigh any fears we may have. Please don't let that important person leave your life without hearing the second element of the blessing—spoken words.

Spoken blessings can also be given for special occasions, such as a birthday, anniversary, graduation, or wedding. You may want to write the words for these blessings so the recipient can keep them as a remembrance, even adding pictures of the event.

Many families have shared their "blessing books" with us. One woman inspired her whole family to write letters of blessing to her parents for their fiftieth wedding anniversary. Each member of the family contributed a letter telling of his or her gratitude, respect, and love for the couple who'd influenced him or her so greatly.

The oldest son in another family, after reading *The Blessing,* involved his brothers and their wives in a project to bless their parents at Christmas. Their blessing presentation included pictures of the families of each of the children, along with words of blessing.

One wrote, "I will always cherish your love and prayerful support. I shall never forget that you used to pray over my pillow. . . . You had been patient with me all through my life, but I knew that you were storming the gates of heaven. I can't help but think that I love to pray because of you."

Each member of this family also chose biblical blessings to add to the presentation. For example, one wrote, "May God grant you, Dad and Mom, your heart's desire. And fulfill all your counsel! We will sing for joy over your victory, and in the name of our God we will set up banners. May the Lord fulfill all your petitions."

The eldest son presented the book on Christmas morning. The parents cried unashamedly as their son read, "This book was prepared with great love. The time and energies expended in preparation of the sections of this book can never repay you for the love, devotion, and blessings the two of you have given to us. This book expresses a sense of blessing toward you in appreciation of your blessings toward us."

A young father prepared words of blessing for his wife and each child. He scripted them on pages with decorated borders. He wrote, in part, "Dearest

Palmer, my firstborn son. I bless you in the name of the Living God and His Son, the Lord Jesus Christ. My heart's desire is that your joy may always be full, that your heart would be overflowing with love, and that your communication with our whole family would be open and rich and full of truth."

Who in your family might need an extra-special blessing celebration?

Who might help you do it?

Take time to plan a strategy. First try to speak, write, or sing words of blessing on a daily basis to those who live in your home. Perhaps once a week you'll choose to write or call loved ones who live elsewhere. You may want to plan a once-a-year blessing celebration for each member of your immediate family.

And what about the third element of the blessing—expressing high value?

A TV show told the story of two foster children who were frequently moved from home to home. In one home, they were sent to their room while the family members ate their dinner of roasted chicken or steak and potatoes or spaghetti or whatever. When the family finished eating, the foster children were allowed into the dining room to eat their portion of . . . beans.

Without words, the children were shown they were of no value to that family. In their next foster home, they were loved—but so much damage had already been done that the younger child, a boy, had developed aggressive behavior. One day he tried to drown his sister in a backyard wading pool. The social worker was called in, and a decision was made to separate the two. The little girl was adopted, but her brother was shunted off to yet another foster home.

The less value he was shown, the more the boy's anger grew, making couples wary of adopting him. In a vicious cycle, this further rejection dropped his self-esteem to an even lower level.

If no one else values us, it's almost impossible to value ourselves.

So what words express high value?

Kristen shows high valuation of her sister with notes at the end of a letter, such as, "You're special. I'm glad you're my sister."

Other words of value might be, "You're important to me," "You mean so much to me," "You made my day!" or "I'm so excited to hear from you."

What words or actions have you used to make the following people feel highly valued?

Your mom

Your dad

A sibling

A teacher

Your spouse

Your children

Have you used devaluing words with these people? What have you said or done recently that may make one of them feel you don't value them highly? (Example: ignoring them when you knew they wanted some of your time.)

How might you be influencing their self-esteem with what you say and do?

When we realize how strongly words affect us, it becomes increasingly clear how important it is to express high value to those we want to bless—and to everyone God puts in our sphere of influence.

FOUR

PICTURING *a* FUTURE *and a* HOPE

LOG ON
Preparing for the Video

Peter and Patti are siblings in their mid-20s. Both are deeply loved by their parents. In most ways, their parents are far above average in giving them the blessing. Both Peter and Patti were given positive-future pictures on short-term activities. Both were encouraged to do their best at whatever they tried.

Patti is one of those relatively rare individuals who knew from childhood what she wanted to be: a doctor. Straight As came easily to her, and she excelled in sports. Her parents are vastly proud of her accomplishments. They encouraged her ambition.

Peter, a year younger, wasn't so fortunate. School wasn't terribly important to him, and grades didn't mean a lot. He liked sports but wasn't a star, and he had no driving ambition for a particular career. His great love was skiing.

Near the end of Patti's junior year in high school, she started applying to colleges. After dinner one night, she excitedly told her aunt and uncle of her plans. Everyone was enthusiastic about her future.

In the midst of the discussion, Peter asked, "What will *I* do? Where should *I* go to college?"

His father answered, "Probably nowhere. You'll just be a ski bum." His words were underlined by his wife's laugh.

The hurt in Peter's eyes was missed by his father and mother. They never dreamed their words caused deep anguish or would have a long-lasting effect. In an attempt not to compare and push Peter to excel as Patti did, his parents didn't expect enough of him.

Each child received a mental picture of his and her future. Patti saw a successful career as a doctor. She may have seen herself in a white jacket, stethoscope dangling from a pocket, striding the halls of a hospital and answering life-or-death calls. Peter's picture—though encompassing the sport he loved—was of a drifting, hollow, non-producing ski bum.

Patti went on to fulfill the future her parents encouraged her to pursue. She's finished medical school.

And Peter? He became a ski bum—just as his father and mother's "hopeless future" words told him he'd be.

SCREEN SHOTS
Watching and Discussing the DVD

After viewing the DVD's Session 4 segment, use questions like the following to help you think through what you saw and heard.

1. Read Jeremiah 29:11, which is addressed to ancient Israel. How do the following Bible characters illustrate God's desire and ability to provide "hope and a future" for individuals?
   • Moses (Exodus 1:22–2:10)
   • Joseph (Genesis 45:4-8)

- Rahab (James 2:25)
- Zaccheus (Luke 19:1-10)

2. How did the bookcase in the apartment of John Trent's mother reflect her hopes for the futures of her sons? How did that affect John? If your bookcase reflected your hopes for your child's or spouse's future, what would it look like?

3. John Trent's mom took a class on genetics and subscribed to a heavy equipment magazine to demonstrate her belief in her boys' future. How could each of the following provide a visible reminder to your child or spouse that you believe in him or her?
   - a bumper sticker
   - a savings bond
   - a calendar
   - a computer screen saver

4. Which of the following statements about your child's future do you think would truly bless him or her? Which might not? Why?
   - "You can grow up to be president."
   - "The country will be bankrupt by the time you get out of college."
   - "You might be the one who discovers a cure for cancer."
   - "If you can dream it, you can do it."
   - "If you become a lawyer, I'll turn over in my grave."

5. What did it cost John Trent's wife, Cindy, to bless their college-bound daughter? How might it cost you something to bless your child, spouse, or friend? How high a price would you be willing to pay?

6. How did John's mom bless her sons by waking up late at night? Why is it important not only to picture a special future for those we want to bless, but also to listen to *their* hopes and dreams about the future?

7. Have you ever known anyone who agreed with the idea of blessing others, but never seemed to get around to doing it? How did this affect that person's loved ones? If the person had made an "active commitment," what difference might it have made?

8. How can you tell when you've made an active commitment to blessing others? If you were to mark that commitment with a ceremony, what would it look like?

9. What's the difference between blessing your child and being a hovering "helicopter parent"? Which do you think is more common in our culture?

10. How could you use the following to teach your child to bless others?
    - a birthday party
    - moving into a new neighborhood
    - moving away from an old neighborhood
    - a heat wave
    - a cold snap
    - a jump in the unemployment rate

11. Why might the devil not be thrilled that you're watching this DVD series? Why might he be even less thrilled if you made an active commitment to blessing specific people?

12. Read James 1:22-25. How can an active commitment to blessing bring blessings to you as well? Read James 2:14-26. When it comes to blessing, have you demonstrated more faith or more action so far? Explain.

LIFE APP
Applying What You've Learned

Picturing a positive future has its negative side. A parent forcing a child into an activity or career of the parent's choosing is not picturing a special future for that child. Such a parent is prescribing a set future for his or her own benefit, not the child's. Our true task is to help our children envision the best possible future they can achieve, not direct them into the career we had or wanted to have.

For example, from the time Jim was able to hold a ball and fit his hand into a glove, his father worked with him to make him a star baseball player. Dad, an ex–major leaguer, was determined that his son would be one, too. Day after day, month after month, year after year, they worked out together. Jim had the talent. He was good.

When he chose a college, Jim went on an academic scholarship, turning down the athletic offers despite his father's anger. He was tired of having to play and practice on every possible occasion, tired of his dad's attempts to control his future. So he dropped out, never playing one more inning.

If your parents planned your future down to a specific college and/or career, did you follow it?

How did that work out?

If your parents didn't plan your future for you, but rather encouraged you to do what your bent led you to, how has that worked out?

If your parents tried to plan your career for you but you resisted and did your own thing, what was the result?

Which of the three options do you think most blesses a person?

The mental pictures our parents or guardians paint for us—whether negative or positive—stay with us, especially if they're repeated over and over. Normally, we do all in our power to make them come true, as author William Glasser, M.D. explains in his book *Control Theory* (Harper and Row, 1985).

According to Glasser, if someone snaps a picture of a future of promise and success and puts it in our mental album, that becomes our motivation to succeed. Likewise, if the future picture is bleak and full of failure, that's the one that will motivate our actions. When a parent says, "You can do it" about the small, daily things in life, it builds confidence for the whole future.

Check the following statements that most closely fit your upbringing.

The future my parents (or other significant person) pictured for me was

___ "You can do anything you set your mind to."

___ "Of course you can pass the test next week. Let's study together."

___ "If you'd only try, you could make something of yourself."

___ "You're so lazy, you'll never amount to anything."

___ "I know you're scared, but you can do it. I believe in you."

___ "We've always had at least one [doctor, lawyer, preacher, teacher] in our family. I guess you're it."

___ "That's a great goal. Go for it."

___ "Okay, the training wheels are off. I'll be right beside you, but you can ride the bike alone."

___ "It's our family business. Of course you're going to take over when I retire."

___ "The way you're going, you don't need to worry about a career. They'll keep you in the State Pen."

___ "With your [musical, sports] talent, you could be a [concert pianist, pro athlete] if you put your heart into it."

___ "Honey, that's a great picture. I'll put it on the fridge door so everyone can see it."

___ "That's too hard. Better go for something you know you can handle."

___ No child of mine is going into such a risky profession. You can be an [electrician, dock worker, teacher, accountant] like your dad."

___ "You're too dumb to have such high aspirations."

___ "If that's what you really want to do, keep plugging away and you'll succeed."

___ "Don't worry about getting through high school now; just concentrate on doing your best in the third grade."

If you have kids, circle the statements that reflect the way you've been picturing their futures.

Finally, if you're married, underline the statements that echo the way you've been treating your spouse's plans and dreams.

Are there any things you'd like to change about your habits in this area?

All of Hank's life, from as early as he can remember, his mother planted in his mind the picture of failure. She said over and over, "You will never amount to anything."

Now 34 years old, Hank says, "I'm bankrupt physically, spiritually, financially, socially, and mentally. How can I reverse these negative word pictures and turn my life around?"

Is this your question, too?

Part of the answer comes from God's already-mentioned declaration in Jeremiah 29:11. Combine it with the promise in Philippians 4:19: "My God will meet all your needs according to his glorious riches in Christ Jesus." God's plan for us gives hope of a special future.

Name three of your strengths. (Example: detailed, persistent, resourceful.)

How might each of these three strengths help others in the future? (Example: With persistence, I could help someone finish an important project.)

Look up Psalm 103 in the Bible. List all the positive things God says about your future.

Now do the same thing with your child's or spouse's strengths.

Next, it's time for that "active commitment"—backing up your words about a special future.

If you've studied the person you want to bless and have found exactly the right special-future words to speak, how will they be received? How much faith will the person put in your words?

The answer depends on how well you do what you say you'll do.

Check the following items that sound like things you've done within the past two years.

_____ "I promised my son I'd take him fishing, but something urgent always came up and we never went."

_____ "I told my daughter I'd look into dance lessons, but never felt it important to follow through."

_____ "I intended to babysit with my nephews so my sister could have an afternoon break, but somehow I never got to it."

_____ "I said I'd see about getting tickets for the football game, and managed to find some. We had a great time!"

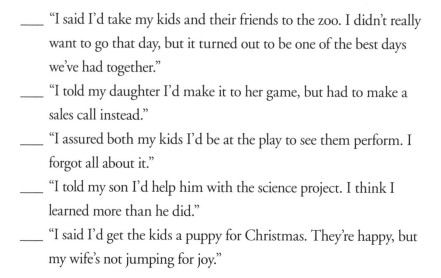

___ "I said I'd take my kids and their friends to the zoo. I didn't really want to go that day, but it turned out to be one of the best days we've had together."

___ "I told my daughter I'd make it to her game, but had to make a sales call instead."

___ "I assured both my kids I'd be at the play to see them perform. I forgot all about it."

___ "I told my son I'd help him with the science project. I think I learned more than he did."

___ "I said I'd get the kids a puppy for Christmas. They're happy, but my wife's not jumping for joy."

Based on your answers, can your children (or others you want to bless) depend on your doing what you say you'll do? Or have they learned to ignore your words because you seldom follow through?

Do you need to work at keeping your word? You can begin today to build the kind of "past" that words of a special future need to rest on by honoring commitments to your children. It may take some time, but with love and perseverance, you can do it.

If you're married, another commitment is vital to assure children of their special futures: your ongoing commitment to your spouse. Words of a special future for a child lose their meaning when a mother or father walks out. The stability of your marriage is directly related to your children's believing you when you say words that picture a special future.

How do you think your children perceive the stability of your marriage?

When you have disagreements, what actions or words might cause your children to worry about the family being split apart?

Do your children have reason to think that divorce might be considered as a solution to family problems?

If yes, how can you change this?

There's one last key to an active commitment to bless our loved ones: making ourselves accountable to someone who will help us continue what we begin.

Genuine commitment to provide the blessing for our loved ones grows best in small groups. You can meet regularly with two or three other parents, siblings, or friends who will ask how you did in blessing others.

With this same group, you can admit your struggles and learn from other people's insights and mistakes. All it takes is the courage to ask honest questions and a loving spirit to share God's truth and your own experiences.

If you're studying *The Blessing* DVD Series with a group, how could group members help you to better bless your children, spouse, parents, and friends?

When will you share that idea with them?

Commitment is costly. Expect to pay a price in . . .

Hard work—providing the blessing to another person;

Time—meaningfully touching those you bless;

Courage—putting into spoken messages words of love that have been on the tip of your tongue;

Wisdom and boldness—highly valuing those you love;

Creativity—picturing a future filled with hope and with God's best.

But all this effort is worthwhile.

That's what Wayne and Peggy found. Their determination to bless their Down syndrome daughter, Sarah Ann, was well worth the work. When Sarah Ann was seven years old, Wayne said, "It's the best seven years of our lives. Sarah Ann is the greatest thing that ever happened to us."

Listen to Hebrews 11:20-21:

"By faith Isaac blessed Jacob and Esau in regard to their future.

"By faith Jacob, when he was dying, blessed each of Joseph's sons, and worshiped as he leaned on the top of his staff."

What will God record about you? What will your children say of you? Will they be so blessed that, like the children of the woman in Proverbs 31, they will rise up and call *you* blessed, too?

FIVE

WHEN *You've* MISSED *the* BLESSING . . .

LOG ON
Preparing for the Video

Many people read self-help books and see themselves in the examples given. They think, *No wonder I'm the way I am. I had dreadful parents and a dysfunctional home.* Some overreact and even put down good parents who tried their best.

But the fact remains that of every ten people you encounter today, five or six probably will have missed out on their parents' blessing. A large segment of our population grew up in homes that withheld it.

If that's true of you, the purpose of discussing these homes isn't to give grounds to blame your parents or guardians. Studying these patterns can lead you to *honor* your parents and take responsibility for how you behave today.

In this session you may discover how to feel compassion for your parents, even if they didn't seem to bless you. You may even find answers to some difficult questions and explanations of your own behaviors that have bothered you. If you find that you need more help, don't hesitate to enlist the aid of a professional Christian counselor. For a referral to a therapist in your area, you can call the Focus on the Family Counseling Department at 1-855-771-4357. We pray that, beginning with this session, you'll begin the healing process.

Families leave a profound mark on every family member. If that mark was constructive, the child does well. If it was destructive and isn't dealt with and forgiven, that child will almost always leave the same harmful mark on his or her own children. People who choose to carry around anger, self-pity, and resentment chain themselves to the past and are likely to repeat it.

Often parents who withhold the blessing lack the knowledge or skill to pass on the blessing. They don't lack love, only the means of showing it. Others do lack love, and their actions can deeply scar their children. When those children reach adulthood, they spend years struggling to escape their past and seldom feel free to enjoy a committed relationship in the present.

What kinds of families tend to withhold the blessing? Here are nine of them.

1. *The home with favoritism.* In this family, one child is favored over the others. One gets a flood of blessing; the others suffer drought.

Ted was the oldest of five brothers—the only one their father cared about. Dad took Ted fishing, kept up on his activities, and gave him all the blessing. After their father died, Ted decided to right things by blessing his brothers. But they totally rejected him—returning the cards he sent on their birthdays and at Christmas, and hanging up on his phone calls. The father's favoritism drove a wedge of resentment between Ted and his brothers that Ted has been unable to remove.

Favoritism can be shown in a variety of ways. In another family the grandmother, who lived in the home, showed her bias by asking the favored child to do all the "little helper" tasks. Some parents heap material gifts on one child because they feel guilty for loving another child more. One mother admitted she was stricter and more demanding of a favorite child. In whatever guise it takes, favoritism cripples the child and withholds the blessing.

2. *The home with over-control.* Margaret's mother is an over-controller. She keeps Margaret toeing her mark with comments like, "I want you to stop right now and think of what it will be like when I'm lying in my casket and you are at my funeral. I want you to imagine sitting there and remembering what an ungrateful, uncaring daughter you were."

The picture is so graphic that Margaret always does whatever her mother wants, to the detriment of her relationships with her husband and children. People like Margaret find early in life that it's not safe to confront or defy. As a result, they may react by letting the controller destroy all other relationships, or by becoming helpless and losing initiative and motivation, or by turning their anger inward and suffering depression.

3. *The home that keeps the blessing just out of reach.* Jim never measured up. He couldn't plow a furrow straight enough to please his father. He couldn't work hard enough or long enough. In an effort to find something he could do well enough to gain his father's approval, he joined the army.

It was 1969, and joining the army for Jim meant going to Vietnam. He'd been in the country less than a week when he was severely wounded in an ambush. He received an honorable discharge and returned to his dad's farm to recuperate.

One day, as he was helping his dad on the farm, Jim walked to where his dad and three other men were talking. One of the farmers told him respectfully, "Jim, we're really proud of you. You fought well for your country, and we're glad to see your wounds are healing okay."

Jim's father snorted. "Don't be proud of my son," he said. "He probably got shot running away from the enemy."

At that moment, Jim realized he would never be able to do anything to satisfy his dad. He was right. His dad never did bless him.

Like Jim, many children spend their lives seeking acceptance because they never quite measured up. They are lured into a futile chase for their parents' affirmation, too bent on their own quest for the blessing to give it to others.

4. *The home with the punishing personality.* There are two types of homes with punishing personalities. One punishes by silence.

Art's dad was like that. He refused to talk with anyone at the dinner table. As a small boy, Art used to sit with tears in his eyes, wondering, *What have I done to make Daddy this way?* Silence communicates a negative message: "I'm here, but you can never come to me."

The other punishing personality uses abuse or anger. Angie's home was a typical example.

When Angie was in high school, she was asked to be an attendant at a friend's wedding. On the big day, full of anticipation, she put on her bridesmaid dress. She was ready to step out the door when her father, drunk and angry, intercepted her. "Where do you think you're going?" he growled.

"Well, Daddy, I'm going to Nancy's wedding. I told you about it."

Angie's father threw his drink at her, splashing most of it on the beautiful dress. She mopped it up as best she could, but arrived at the wedding smelling like a brewery. The happy occasion turned into a hurtful experience with lasting consequences.

5. *The home that exchanges blessing for a burden.* In this home, a terrible transaction takes place. A child is coaxed by guilt or fear into giving up all rights to his or her goals and desires. Instead of living his or her own life, the child does what the parent demands. In return, the child gets a blessing that lasts until the next time the parent manipulates him or her to fulfill the parent's desires. If the child never breaks free, he loses his identity and spends his life enslaved to following what his parent demands.

Bob's parents owned an auto supply store and expected Bob to take over the business when Dad retired. Bob kept his father's blessing—as long as he worked at the store. When Bob decided God wanted him to cut back his hours and study for the ministry, his father banged his fist on the counter and yelled, "The store's not good enough for you, huh? Well, I'll show you. You don't have to work. Not at all. You're fired!" He refused to help Bob in any way, financially or by giving him the blessing.

Parents who attach strings to the blessing do their children a grave disservice. A blessing is a gift, not something that needs to be earned. Like God's love, it's an act of unmerited favor and unconditional acceptance bestowed upon a person of high value.

6. *The home with emotional minefields.* These are often, but not always, the homes of alcoholics.

When Andy was ten, he came home from school one afternoon and, leaving his chores undone, went out to play with friends. Later he saw his dad drive up and ran toward him, eager to say hello.

Dad opened the door, stepped out of the car, and, without a word, swung a fist at Andy and knocked him out. Moments later, when the boy came to, his dad jerked him up and yelled at him for not doing his chores. Andy didn't know that he'd upset his mom, who'd called his dad and complained. "That was almost 30 years ago," Andy says. "But I can still remember how my jaw hurt."

That's an emotional minefield. Andy never knew when the next punch might come.

Minefields create fear and distrust. The Bible tells us, "There is no fear in love. But perfect love drives out fear" (1 John 4:18). The reverse is also true. Fear has the capacity to drive out love, so the more fear you have, the less loving—and the less interested in blessing others—you'll be.

7. *The home with unyielding family traditions.* In Kyle's family, the oldest son for generations has been a minister or doctor or lawyer, so Kyle's oldest son is expected to be one too. No one in Martha's family has ever married outside his or her social class, so Martha's daughters are expected to follow the tradition. If Janet doesn't pledge the right sorority, her mother will withhold the blessing.

Parents who do this know full well the impact of withholding their blessing; that's exactly why they do it. Their expectations have been dashed, and they want their son or daughter to hurt as well.

Children who miss the blessing because they broke an ironclad family tradition often feel emotionally bankrupt. They can find no way to please their parents and restore the blessing.

8. *The home with secrets.* Family secrets are meant to "protect" everyone in the home. If no outsider knows that Uncle George committed suicide or that Suzie had an abortion, the family is "safe."

But by keeping secrets, family members place each other in jeopardy. If the secret is that Mom is addicted to painkillers, for instance, she's less likely to get help. They may also miss the chance to give and receive the blessing.

That was the case in Ralph's home. Ralph had invited his father, now elderly and ill, to live with him and his wife. Not long after his father moved in, Ralph lost his job. Ralph and his wife decided it would be best not to worry his father, so they instructed the kids not to tell.

It wasn't long before Ralph's father's health deteriorated. The doctor who examined him said, "You know, there's something else going on. Something besides a physical ailment."

"Yeah," said Dad. "I don't know what it is, but something's wrong with my son. It's eating me alive, tearing me up inside. I can't sleep at night."

The doctor called Ralph in from the waiting room and said, "Let's have it out. What's going on that's bothering your father so much?"

Ralph looked at his dad, drew a deep breath, and said, "I lost my job. I didn't want you to worry, so I couldn't tell you."

"Lost your job?" his dad cried. "That's wonderful! I thought something was *really* wrong. I lost my job when I was your age. I remember it was tough for a while, but we made it. Why didn't you tell me, son? I could help." This family secret had kept Ralph from the blessing of being comforted by his father.

9. *The home that offers only part of the blessing.* Three common situations in which this occurs are divorce, desertion, and adoption.

In a typical divorce, the mother has custody of the children and the father has visitation rights. Early on, the father lavishes attention on the children, but as the months go by, contact begins to decrease. By the time three years have passed, many fathers see their children once a month or less. As the visits decrease in frequency and duration, the children feel increasingly angry and insecure.

Seven months after Danny's parents divorced, his dad quit coming so often. The gifts stopped. Danny's dad was now living with the woman he'd left Danny's mom for and becoming more and more involved with her two children. He no longer kept his word that "nothing would change."

The blessing a father gives his child is as important as the blessing of the mother. When it's absent, there's a vacuum in the child's life that needs to be filled.

Desertion by a parent can be harder on a child than losing him or her to death. When a parent dies, a child knows that in this life the opportunity to regain a missing part of the blessing from that parent is gone. When a parent deserts his or her children, they know that "out there somewhere" is a living person who still has the power to bless.

That was the case with Gene, whose father left one day when Gene was about three years old. Gene cried himself to sleep many nights, wondering if he'd done something terribly wrong to cause his dad not to come home.

Many years later, when Gene was an adult and working as a salesman for a farm machine company, he attended a national sales meeting. One of the other salesmen walked up to him and said, "Yours is an unusual last name. A guy who lives on our block in Atlanta has the same name. Any relation?"

Gene didn't know, but decided to call the man who bore his name. After a bit of preliminary conversation, Gene said, "You know, I think I'm your son. I'd like to reestablish contact. I'd love to introduce you to my family."

His father responded with a rejection. "I left for a reason. I didn't want any part of you or anyone else in your mother's family. I'm not interested in seeing you, and I don't want you to call any more."

Gene was devastated all over again. That lifelong hope that sometime, somewhere, he'd find his father and get the blessing died.

A third group of children who commonly struggle with gaining only part of the blessing is adoptees who ask, "Why did my biological parents leave me?" The question comes up even in homes where the child is secure in his or her adoptive parents' love.

Many feel compelled to seek their biological parents in an attempt to regain that part of the blessing they lost. Adoptive parents can provide about 95 percent of a missing blessing for an adopted child, but there is still 5 percent they can't, no matter how much the child is loved. That 5 percent may be filled if a child and birth parent are reunited and the birth parent gives the blessing. If that never happens, the 5 percent can also be filled by a relationship with God through Jesus Christ.

So what happens when you miss the blessing?

The answer depends on individual circumstances—the way the blessing was withheld, how much was withheld, and the personality traits of the parent and the child who missed the blessing.

We've discovered seven common effects of missing the blessing. As you read through the following descriptions of those who suffer the effects, consider which might apply to you.

1. *Seekers.* These people search for intimacy, but are seldom able to tolerate it. They feel tremendous fulfillment in the thrill of courtship. But after marriage, they chafe at the close relationship. Lack of acceptance from their parents has made them uncomfortable in receiving love and approval from a spouse. Though a spouse might compensate for almost 80 percent of a missed parental blessing, a seeker is unable to accept even that much.

2. *The Shattered.* Shattered people live with fear, anxiety, depression, and emotional withdrawal. The shattered person's unhappy road can even lead to the terrifying cliffs of suicide, because those who are shattered are convinced they are destined to be nonentities.

3. *Smotherers.* Like giant sponges, smotherers react to not getting their parents' blessing by absorbing every bit of life and energy from a spouse, child, friend, or entire congregation. A smotherer is so emotionally empty that he or she drains others of their desire to listen or help. Smotherers end up pushing away the blessing other people might offer, and are unlikely to offer blessings themselves.

4. *The Angry.* People who are angry are shackled to the objects of their anger. Many adults, angry over missing the blessing, are still emotionally chained to their parents. Having never forgiven nor forgotten, they're distracted from intimacy by the rattle of emotional chains.

Marsha is a good example. Her two stepdaughters unwittingly did something that made her furious. She wrote to both with raging comments. Both girls apologized and tried to set matters straight, but Marsha refused to surrender her anger.

When the girls visit their father, Marsha disappears into her bedroom until they leave. She refuses to communicate with them in any way. She even weakens her relationship with their father in order to nurse her anger. Needless to say, Marsha is not blessing her family.

5. *The Detached.* Rodney was a sensitive boy who loved art and creating things. After his dad died, his mother remarried. Rodney's stepdad was harsh and unloving, totally different from his father. In self-defense, Rodney cut himself off from all feelings. He gave up creative pursuits and became a CPA, a career that seemed to require a clinical, straightforward personality.

When Rodney's wife complained that he never expressed his emotions to her, that he never said, "I love you" or "I care for you," Rodney agreed to seek counseling. During one session he said, "I don't think I have ever had any feelings for my wife. I buried feelings a long time ago and don't feel anything. I don't feel love. I don't feel anger. Those all died when my stepfather took over my life." He turned to his wife and added, "I do love you in my own way, but I don't feel."

Like Rodney, many spend their lives protecting themselves from being hurt again. Their detachment comes at the price of loneliness and being unable to bless others.

6. *The Driven.* In this category, line up extreme perfectionists, workaholics, and notoriously picky housecleaners. They go after the blessing by trying to earn it. The problem is that the blessing is a gift; you can't buy it.

Missing their parents' blessing challenges these driven people to attack a windmill named "accomplishment" in an illusory attempt to gain love and acceptance.

Take Terry, for example. She was hired by a national firm as a first-level manager. But she knew she wouldn't measure up to her dad's standards if she stayed at first-line management for long, so she began spending up to 12 hours a day on the job. She won her promotion—but eventually lost her marriage and the chance to ever bless her husband again.

7. *The Seduced.* Many who have missed out on their parents' blessing look for that lost love in all the wrong places.

When Ardis was only five or six, her mother would come into her room early in the morning to see whether the girl had hung her clothes up properly the night before. If not, the woman would jerk every garment out of the closet, wake up Ardis, and make her hang everything up right.

Ardis's father did nothing to stop this abuse. When the girl reached high school, she sought love to fill up the vast emptiness inside her. As soon as a boy was kind or showed her any warmth, she practically fell into his arms. She continued that pattern in high school and college, trying to fill her unmet needs for love and acceptance.

Substance abusers also fall into this category. Addictions can begin with attempts to cover up the hurt from empty relationships. From drug abuse to compulsive gambling, these behaviors can become counterfeit ways to try to gain the deep emotional warmth of the blessing. And those whose lives are consumed by addictions have little energy left for blessing others.

If you missed the blessing, do you see yourself and your past in any of these categories? If so, your future can be different. Resolution comes when we turn to our heavenly Father for His blessing and then learn to bless others.

SCREEN SHOTS
Watching and Discussing the DVD

After viewing the DVD's Session 5 segment, use questions like the following to help you think through what you saw and heard.

1. On a scale of 1 to 10 (10 being most serious), how serious a problem do you think it is when someone misses the blessing? How would you compare it to the following problems?
    - growing up in poverty
    - having parents who divorced
    - being a victim of cyber-bullying
    - having a speech impediment

2. Do you know anyone who seemed to become richer, more competitive, better known, or more physically fit because he or she missed the blessing? If so, does that mean missing the blessing can be a good thing? Why or why not?

3. What percentage of the people featured in this video segment seem to have missed the blessing? Do you think that's higher than, lower than, or about the same as in the general population?

4. How would you summarize the advice in this video for those who've missed the blessing?
   - "You'll never be normal."
   - "Get over it."
   - "You can overcome it."
   - "Turn to God for help."
   - other _____

5. Most of the attention in this video segment is given to those whose parents failed to bless them. In each of the following pairs, though, how might the first person withhold the blessing from the second? What might the effects be?
   - a husband and a wife
   - a sister and a brother
   - a supervisor and an employee
   - a child and a parent

6. How perfectly does a parent have to bless his or her child in order to avoid the "failure to bless" label? How can you tell whether you're blessing your child enough?

7. John Trent missed his father's blessing. How do you think John overcame that?
   - by being in denial about it
   - by letting his mother's blessing make up for it
   - by being mentored by other caring adults

- by becoming a Christian and relying on God's blessing
- by becoming a counselor and writing a book on the subject
- other _____

8. Is it necessary to have received the blessing in order to bless someone else? Why or why not?

9. If the following were real crimes, what punishments might be appropriate?
    - withholding the blessing from a minor child
    - failure to bless a spouse
    - blessing for the purpose of controlling an adult child

10. Read Genesis 32:24-30. How was Jacob's experience of "wrestling for a blessing" like that of some people who weren't blessed as children? How was it different?

11. If there were an organization called Blessing Missers Anonymous, what might be the first three steps of its twelve-step program? Do you think such an organization would be effective? Why or why not?

12. As a result of watching this video, which of the following do you most want to do? Why?
    - bless your child
    - feel sorry for yourself
    - write someone an angry e-mail
    - make an appointment with a therapist
    - forgive your parents
    - other _____

LIFE APP
Applying What You've Learned

Remember the nine kinds of homes that withhold the blessing? Which of them, if any, did you come from?

____ one where favoritism was shown

____ one in which a parent exercised too much control

____ one in which the blessing was just out of reach

____ one with punishing personalities

____ one in which blessings were purchased with burdens

____ one with emotional minefields

____ one with unyielding family traditions

____ one that kept secrets

____ one with partial blessings

How do you feel about that?

How do you think that experience affected your ability to receive the blessing? To bless others?

Have you ever confronted someone you felt failed to bless you? If not, why not? If so, what happened?

Have you ever forgiven someone you felt failed to bless you? If not, why not? If so, what happened?

Help and hope are available for those who grew up in these family situations. With a healthy attitude and the right information, you can find a path from the ranks of the unblessed to the ranks of the blessed—though that path may not be short or easy.

Every one of the elements of the blessing you may have missed can be yours from your heavenly Father. The journey begins by discovering the reality of a relationship that God holds out to everyone through Jesus Christ, and by being willing to courageously face the past.

In an article in *Newsweek* ("Too Late to Say, 'I'm Sorry,'" August 31, 1987), Joseph M. Queenan recalled his miserable years of growing up with an alcoholic father. Three years before he wrote the article, his father, then a recovering alcoholic, came to him and apologized. He said to Queenan, "Son, I'm sorry for anything I may have done to harm you."

Queenan rejected the apology, resenting the words "may have done" and what he felt to be an almost ritualistic tendering of the apology—as if it were an assignment rather than prompted by real feeling. He'd hated his father for the first 20 years of his life, but said he didn't hate him anymore because he'd looked into his father's past. His father had also had an alcoholic father, had grown up during the Depression, was a high school dropout, had served an 18-month prison term for going AWOL to attend his mother's funeral, and had four children he couldn't support.

Instead of feeling compassion for his father, Queenan wrote, "I wish him well, but I don't want to see him. I understand, but I won't forgive. It's too late to say, 'I'm sorry.'"

Is it ever too late?

Queenan made some good choices—and some bad ones. He made the effort to understand his father, but refused to forgive him.

So what should we do if we've missed the blessing?

The sooner we come to grips with the fact that we may never get the blessing from those who seem not to have it to give, the sooner we can turn our energies to other pursuits. We need to deal with our pain and grief and get on with our lives.

1. *Face up to the problem.* Examine your feelings and memories to see how much you believe you were blessed or missed the blessing. Regardless of the facts, the perception of having been blessed or not blessed is the reality you feel.

Though it may be painful to dredge up hurtful memories, only in facing them can we begin the healing process. For some, understanding why they feel as they do is enough to set them on the track to healing.

Jackie wrote, "I felt once again totally rejected and went through a period of depression. Eventually, I just gave all of my grief to my heavenly Father. That is, until I read *The Blessing* and discovered my underlying problem. I can now begin to go about my life with the understanding of my search for the blessing. I want more than anything to break the chain and to bless my children."

How have you reacted to a lack of blessing? Check any statements that apply to you.

_____ I feel that I just exist; my life is not significant.

_____ I'm afraid of being disloyal, so I hold my hurt inside, refusing to admit it.

_____ Most relationships in my life are negative.

_____ I have a deep sense of inferiority.

_____ I'm angry, like Queenan, and refuse to forgive.

_____ Like my parents, I did not give my children the blessing—so I've messed up their lives, too.

_____ I usually give my kids what I wanted and didn't get.

____ I hope my spouse, job, possessions, or a move to a new place will fill the gap I sense in my heart.

____ I expect God to supply my needs.

Which of these responses do you think are positive and lead to healing?

Which will only dig you deeper into anger and lack of self-esteem?

Based on your replies to the above exercise, how much healing do you think needs to be done in your life?

2. *Understand your parents' background.* Part of the healing process comes when we know why our parents acted the way they did. Queenan discovered several mitigating facts about his father that explained why he did what he did. We need to do the same thing.

Begin searching out your parents' history. Contact your aunts and uncles if you have some. Ask them questions about your mother's or father's childhood. Look through old family photo albums for clues. If anyone in the family kept a journal with relevant information he or she is willing to share, include that, too. Summarize here what you find out.

How does the information you've uncovered help you understand why your parents acted as they did?

If your parent died before you were old enough to remember him or her, the following may help.

As you do your research, take pictures of your parent's home, the schools he or she went to, his or her family members who are still living, places he or she probably visited. Put together a physical or digital photo album that reflects what his or her life was like, annotated with comments from relatives and friends.

If possible, visit your parent's grave. Take pictures of the headstone or marker and the surroundings. Perhaps have someone take a picture of you standing by the headstone.

Finally, write yourself a letter of blessing from that parent, using the information you've gleaned. Write it as you honestly think he or she might have given you the blessing had he or she lived longer. You can use the space below to write down some ideas for this blessing.

3. *Forgive.* Healing depends on our willingness to forgive those who've hurt us. If you, like Queenan, choose not to forgive, you'll spend the rest of your life fighting the results of having missed the blessing. On the other hand, if you forgive, the hurt feelings can be put behind, and you can find a fulfilling

life. This doesn't mean forgiveness is simple or speedy, or that you're condoning the way you were treated. It means you're taking a first step toward freeing yourself from the burden of having to retaliate.

We've shared elsewhere the story of Denny, an angry young man who threw his abusive father out a second story window. He eventually came to forgive his father and even had the joy of leading him to Christ. He also had the joy of seeing most of his family forgive his father and find freedom—all but one sister.

After Denny had taken his father to her home to ask forgiveness, she wrote:

> Father, your coming to see me was an outrage! There is no way you can come and preach forgiveness to me after all the scars I bear from you. For years, you have been all I have thought about. My every word, each decision I have made.
>
> You have been responsible for my becoming a prostitute.
>
> You are responsible for my marriage that broke up. You are the reason I have had an operation so I can never have children—I'm afraid of what I'd do to them. You ask me to forgive you? You are not to be forgiven. You are to be conquered. If it takes me the rest of my life, I'll bury your memory. Don't ever call or come to see me again.

Denny is free and at peace. But his sister's life has been controlled by hatred and bitterness for years because she made a decision out of her hurt to treat others with as little value as she herself received. She devalues God. She is blind to how much God values her. She dishonors her father's memory, and remains in emotional and spiritual chains.

Healing comes with forgiveness. The following Bible verses deal with that subject. Underscore or highlight the words that reveal God's standard of forgiveness. Then write, in your own words, what the verse says about your need to forgive others. The first verse is done as a sample for you to follow.

"For if you <u>forgive men when they sin against you</u>, <u>your heavenly Father will also forgive you</u>" (Matthew 6:14). (*My forgiveness from God depends on my forgiving others.*)

Then Peter came to Jesus and asked, 'Lord, how many times shall I forgive my brother when he sins against me? Up to seven times?'

"Jesus answered, 'I tell you, not seven times, but seventy-seven times'" (Matthew 18:21-22).

"And when you stand praying, if you hold anything against anyone, forgive him, so that your Father in heaven may forgive you your sins" (Mark 11:25).

"Be kind and compassionate to one another, forgiving each other, just as in Christ God forgave you" (Ephesians 4:32).

"Bear with each other and forgive whatever grievances you may have against one another. Forgive as the Lord forgave you" (Colossians 3:13).

Forgiveness, like love, is a decision we make. It's not impossible if we pray for God's help and determine we're going to do it. It will most likely be painful.

List, in order of difficulty, three things you find hardest to forgive.

Why are these things so difficult to forgive?

If you have sisters or brothers who also feel the lack of blessing, ask them what is most difficult for them to forgive and why. How do their answers compare with yours?

What have you decided about forgiving those who failed to bless you?

If those people are living, how and when will you contact them to tell them you forgive them? What do you need to say?

If your parents are no longer living, write out your statement of forgiveness anyway. Give a copy to your spouse or a friend to read. This will help to provide a feeling of having completed the task.

4. *Honor your parents.* Forgiving is the first step in honoring our parents. But it is only the first step. We must go on to give them the honor God requires (Leviticus 19:3; Deuteronomy 27:16; Matthew 15:4; Ephesians 6:2).

Proverbs 20:20 states, "If a man curses his father or mother, his lamp will be snuffed out in pitch darkness." A curse may be defined as valuing lightly, below actual worth; to dishonor or despise. If your perception of your parents is that they dishonored you, three Bible verses may help you on the way to healing.

"However, the Lord your God would not listen to Balaam but turned the curse into a blessing for you, because the Lord your God loves you" (Deuteronomy 23:5).

"It may be that the Lord will see my distress and repay me with good for the cursing I am receiving today" (2 Samuel 16:12).

"Like a fluttering sparrow or a darting swallow, an undeserved curse does not come to rest" (Proverbs 26:2).

Though our dishonoring actions may cause pain to our parents, they cause far deeper, longer lasting problems for us. They keep us from being free to be the people God designed us to be.

We need to begin now, but don't expect the process to be over in a day or two. Healing may take months, even years, to complete. We weren't hurt in a single instant, and healing won't happen that fast.

If your hurts are deep, like those of Denny's sister, you may need to go beyond the scope of this DVD series and seek professional counseling. Don't let anything keep you from doing what's necessary to find the healing you need.

SIX

BRINGING *the* BLESSING HOME— *and* BEYOND

LOG ON
Preparing for the Video

At the end of a class I (John Trent) was teaching, one woman handed me this note: *Dennis has learned so much about how to "bless" the children. It has made a real difference in his relationship with them. How about teaching him how to bless me!!*

This woman's request was right on target. The elements of the blessing aren't limited to the parent-child relationship. They're essential as the heart of *any* healthy relationship.

So let's consider *all* the people we need to bless.

1. *Our children.* Old Testament fathers did this; Jesus did, too.

Blessing our children needn't be a grand production. It can be quite simple. For example, my (John's) daughter Kari had a dance recital coming up. For several months she practiced diligently at her weekly dance class and what seemed like *daily* at home.

Finally, when the dance recital was only one week away, Kari came down with chicken pox.

Too sick to dance and too sad to talk about her disappointment without crying, Kari was heartbroken that Saturday. That is, until the doorbell rang for her. It was a deliveryman with a simple "pick-me-up" bouquet, complete with flowers and balloons. The message that came with it she still keeps in her desk drawer: "Even though you didn't get to dance today, you're still our favorite dancer. We love you very much. Mom and Dad."

It took all of three minutes for me to order those flowers, but it made her whole weekend. And in the years to come, it will provide just one more reminder that every day, even on those days full of disappointment and hurt, she has Mom and Dad's blessing.

2. *Our spouse.* When Cindy and I (John) were first married, I'd finished my master's degree and was applying to various schools to go on for my doctorate. I felt confident that I'd have my choice of schools. But one school in particular topped my list. Finally, a response came from this university. I opened the letter and began reading it to Cindy.

It wasn't until I was three-fourths of the way through the letter that it dawned on me that this was a *rejection* letter, not an acceptance. I faltered to a stop, all too conscious of my new bride hearing this unexpected humiliation. I felt like a failure.

I stuffed the letter into my pocket and said, "Guess I'd better get off to work. I don't want to be late."

When I returned home that night, Cindy had a favorite dinner waiting for me. Beside my plate was a scroll tied with ribbon. Opening it, I read Cindy's handwritten message: *It's OK that this school rejected you. Even if every school turns you down, it won't make any difference. I'll still love you. God will still use you to help other people. Your life will be blessed.*

Cindy hugged me and whispered, "It's okay, you know. I love you."

What is your spouse feeling right now that could be helped or healed by a touch, a word, or a gesture from you that shows unconditional love?

3. *Our parents.* Many of our parents need our blessing. We can't completely fill their cup of missed blessing, but we can start the flow and let our heavenly Father fill it up.

Ruth had missed out on the blessing from her parents. Her father died when she was very young, and her mother didn't know how to pass on a blessing she'd never received.

Unfortunately, she also did not receive the blessing from her husband. She spent her life seeking love, but never believing that anyone really loved her.

Her four children decided that they'd plan an eightieth birthday party as a blessing for their mother so she'd know how much she was loved. They planned carefully, even having all her friends mail their cards to the oldest daughter's home to be put into a scrapbook.

The celebration was held in the fellowship hall of Ruth's church, and it was packed. Before the birthday cake was cut, Ruth's children each spoke a word of blessing, then presented their mother with the scrapbook containing all the cards—plus letters of blessing from each of them.

Ruth still struggled with feeling blessed in later years. But for at least that one day, she knew beyond a doubt that she was loved.

4. *Our friends.* The best-known Bible story of friend blessing friend is David and Jonathan. Though Jonathan had every reason to hate David, he loved him and chose to bless him. When his father, King Saul, threatened harm to David, Jonathan warned him and asked God to call David's enemies to account (1 Samuel 20:13-17).

Brock had friends like Jonathan—four of them. They worked with him and cared when they saw he was having trouble in his marriage and with life in general. The four were going to a Promise Keepers seminar, and decided they'd take Brock with them. Like the men who lowered the paralytic down through the roof to get to Jesus, they approached Brock and said, "There's a great conference next week that's designed to help men make a go of their marriages and family. We're all going. We're going to take you along."

Brock said, "Thanks, fellas, but I can't. Things are just too tight at home. We can't afford it."

"We're paying the way, and you're riding with us."

Brock hedged. "I'm not sure how Diana would feel about it."

"We've already checked with her. She thinks it's great. You're going."

Smiling, Brock agreed. "I'd love to."

He liked these guys. On the way to the conference, they talked to him about his need to have Christ in his life. Just hours before the conference began, Brock became a new Christian. Later he met regularly with his four friends, who helped him grow in his newfound faith and in learning to bless his family as his friends had blessed him.

5. *Our neighbors.* Jesus told us to love our neighbors as ourselves. He clearly showed that anyone He brings into our lives needing help, comfort, or material goods is our neighbor.

That includes the clerk at the grocery store, the mail deliverer, the old curmudgeon across the street who's always yelling at your children, and the people you work with. We can look at each and ask, "What can I do to give at least one element of the blessing to this person?" It may be no more than a smile. It could be a ride to the doctor's office. It might be telling the person about Jesus.

Consider your schedule for the rest of the day. How many people will you meet who need the blessing?

SCREEN SHOTS
Watching and Discussing the DVD

1. Which of the people featured in this video segment do you think has received the greatest benefit from the blessing? Why? If you could ask that person a question, what would it be?

2. If you had been interviewed for this video, what might you have said about the blessing? How would you hope people would respond?

3. Which of the following would you most like to see interviewed about the benefits of the blessing? Why?
   - Jacob and Esau
   - one of the children who was blessed personally by Jesus
   - your spouse
   - your children
   - other _____

4. Following through on the blessing often takes a long-term commitment. Under which of the following circumstances would you be tempted to withdraw your blessing? How do you think you'd actually handle each situation?
   - Your teenage son decides he wants to be a hedge fund manager instead of a missionary.
   - Your 22-year-old daughter moves in with her boyfriend.
   - Your spouse admits that he or she has lost $2,000 in online gambling.
   - Your five-year-old son declares that he hates you.
   - Your father has an affair and your mother divorces him.

5. John Trent warns that if you've neglected your loved ones and suddenly try to bless them, you may encounter skepticism or resistance. How would you overcome that in each of the following cases?
   - Your spouse has seen you get "fired up" about spiritual things before, only to forget about them when the "mountaintop experience" is over.

- You've rarely touched your child except to administer spankings, and now you want to use appropriate, meaningful touch to convey a blessing.
- You've always told your underachieving middle child that he'll "end up flipping burgers," and now you have to picture a special future for him.

6. Have you ever seen a blessing "reverse the curse"? If so, what happened?

7. On a scale of 1 to 10 (10 highest), how hard would it be for you to bless each of the following? Do you think God wants you to bless these people anyway? Why or why not?
   - someone who bullied you when you were a child
   - a terrorist
   - someone who owes you $500
   - your least favorite relative

8. On a scale of 1 to 10 (10 highest), how good is your church at blessing people? How good is it at equipping you to bless others? What's one thing you could do to improve these scores?

9. Who needs your blessing most urgently? How could the following categories help you decide?
   - someone no one else is likely to bless
   - someone whose health could shorten his or her life
   - someone who's been "cursed" in the past
   - someone for whom you're responsible
   - someone who's depressed or suicidal
   - other _____

10. If you wanted to motivate one million people to bless their children, how would you do it?
    - give each of them a "blessing coin"
    - pay them $100 each
    - show them this DVD series
    - tell them your own story
    - other _____

11. As you wrap up this course, what's the single most important thing you've learned about the blessing?

12. What do you hope you'll be able to say one year from now as a result of participating in this course? What do you hope *won't* happen?

LIFE APP
Applying What You've Learned

How big can the circle of blessing become? Is it possible that if we included too many people, our blessing would be spread so thin that we wouldn't really bless anyone?

It could happen. So we set priorities. We focus the blessing where we have the greatest responsibility and then spread the blessing as far as God enables us.

1. *The Inner Circle.* Your immediate family is your spouse and children if you're married; if you're unmarried, perhaps it's your siblings or substitute family. They get the bulk of your attention. They need daily doses of all the blessing's elements from you.

Singer Mel Tillis had over twenty number-one hits on the country bestseller charts. Yet he said, "My five kids tell me I'm number one on their list. That's better than any bestseller list, anytime."

We start with those people closest to us, and when we're sure we're number one on their list, then we branch out to others.

2. *The Second Circle.* The extended family—parents, siblings, and other family members—is second in priority to hear words of praise and commendation from you.

The first commandment with a promise is "Honor your father and your mother" (Exodus 20:12). According to Ephesians 6:2-3, we're to obey this command "that it may go well with you and that you may enjoy long life on the earth." Honor is synonymous with blessing in Scripture, so we must bless our parents.

Brothers and sisters, perhaps cousins, grandparents, and others related by blood or marriage, fall into this category.

3. *The Third Circle.* The family of believers is Christians. Many of them have not received the blessing; you can bless them using some of the biblical elements. Galatians 6:10 says, "Therefore, as we have opportunity, let us do good to all people, especially to those who belong to the family of believers."

As you grow older and your children leave home, you may have time and energy to be a surrogate parent, one who blesses younger Christians in your church. As Paul instructed Titus, we can teach older men to be temperate, teach older women to teach what is good to younger women, and encourage younger men to be self-controlled (Titus 2:1-6).

God provides a spiritual family—other believers who become like brothers and sisters, fathers and mothers, aunts and uncles. These people are available to help meet our needs. God knows our need for meaningful touch and for the physical companionship of others to build up our lives and encourage us, and this is the way He has chosen to provide.

Fae, like many others, received the elements of the blessing from a spiritual "mother." She says, "God has given me at least one person in my life who has blessed me. Neither of my parents ever gave me or my brothers the family blessing. I grew up hurting.

"Then I met a Sunday school teacher. Although my mother never went to church, she allowed me to go to Sunday school with a neighbor girl. I'd only gone a couple of weeks, so I was surprised when Miss Joscelyn's eyes lit up when I walked into the room that third week. She began giving me hugs each Sunday, and she'd ask about how my week had been. She was like a spiritual mother to me and made a tremendous difference in my life. I'll never forget her."

Who from God's spiritual family has entered your life to bless you as the Sunday school teacher did Fae?

What has he or she done?

What has been the result in your life?

If you could choose a spiritual sister, brother, mother, or father, what qualifications would you look for?

Where might you meet a spiritual family member to bless you?

_____ a small group or Sunday school class

_____ a church singles group, if you're single

_____ a men's or women's group in the church

_____ other _____

Whether or not you've been blessed by a spiritual sister or brother, have you considered blessing others?

Who might you choose from your spiritual family to bless? Why?

What could you do to bless him or her?

One woman attending a large church decided to help others in the spiritual family to give at least a part of the blessing. She designed a form like this one:

Name _____

I saw Jesus in you today when you . . .

_____

_____

_____

She made copies on half sheets of pastel paper and made them available to everyone in her church. Anyone could pick up a supply, fill them out, and give or send them to the ones he or she wanted to bless.

They were very effective. Jan used one to express the blessing she'd felt from a new business acquaintance. The woman responded with a note to say that the message was just what she needed to lift her spirits after a particularly difficult day.

4. *The Outer Circle.* "All people" (Galatians 6:10) includes those God brings into our lives in divine encounters. These may be few, and you may do much less with them than you would with the first three circles.

Who are some people in this category whom you need to bless?

How and when do you need to bless them?

When it comes to giving the blessing—no matter which circle is involved—do it now!

Sam had grown up in a home that withheld the blessing. When he had sons, he didn't know how to bless them. One day he heard about *The Blessing.* He picked up a copy and realized this was what he'd missed, and he needed to start blessing his children.

Shortly after reading *The Blessing,* he took his 14-year-old son, Mike, with him to meet an old buddy who was a stunt pilot. While Mike watched, Sam and his best buddy took off to do some air ballet and stunts. In the middle of a loop, where the plane was supposed to head straight up and then fall over backward, the pilot made an error. He didn't have enough altitude to correct, and the plane crashed to the tarmac.

Mike rushed over and dragged out the pilot, who appeared to be all right. Mike struggled frantically to get his dad out of the plane; by the time he succeeded, he realized his dad was going to die. Sam knew it, too.

Immediately, Sam reached out and took Mike's hand. In the 45 minutes before he died, Sam gave all five elements of the blessing to Mike. He touched him, gave him a verbal message expressing high value and a promising future, and spent his last minutes in commitment to blessing his son.

Unfortunately, most of us think we've got 45 years left—that there's a lot of time for us to give the blessing. So we procrastinate.

Are you putting off blessing your children, your spouse, friends, neighbors, all people?

Write down the name of a person you can trust to help keep you accountable for carrying out your blessing goals.

Ask him or her to contact you on a regular basis to see if you've done what you plan. Better yet, form a small group of people who are interested in giving the blessing—and become accountable to the group.

Don't miss the blessing . . . of *being* a blessing.

ABOUT THE AUTHORS

Dr. John Trent is president of the Center for Strong Families and founder of StrongFamilies.com. He speaks at conferences across the country and has authored or coauthored more than a dozen award-winning and bestselling books. Along with Focus on the Family, he recently launched The Blessing Challenge, a seven-year initiative with the goal of helping one million people choose to change the life of one child (find out more at www.TheBlessing.com). John and his wife, Cindy, have been married for more than thirty years and have two grown daughters.

Gary Smalley is one of America's best-known authors and speakers on family relationships. He is the author or coauthor of 28 award-winning and bestselling books including *The DNA of Relationships*. He has appeared on TV programs including *The Today Show*, *Oprah*, and *Larry King Live* as well as many national radio programs. Gary is the founder of the Smalley Relationship Center. He and his wife, Norma, have been married for more than forty years and have three grown children.

FOCUS ON THE FAMILY®

Welcome to the Family

Whether you purchased this book, borrowed it, or received it as a gift, thanks for reading it! This is just one of many insightful, biblically based resources that Focus on the Family produces for people in all stages of life.

Focus is a global Christian ministry dedicated to helping families thrive as they celebrate and cultivate God's design for marriage and experience the adventure of parenthood. Our outreach exists to support individuals and families in the joys and challenges they face, and to equip and empower them to be the best they can be.

Through our many media outlets, we offer help and hope, promote moral values and share the life-changing message of Jesus Christ with people around the world.

Focus on the Family
MAGAZINES

These faith-building, character-developing publications address the interests, issues, concerns, and challenges faced by every member of your family from preschool through the senior years.

For More
INFORMATION

ONLINE:
Log on to
FocusOnTheFamily.com
In Canada, log on to
FocusOnTheFamily.ca

PHONE:
Call toll-free:
**800-A-FAMILY
(232-6459)**
In Canada, call toll-free:
800-661-9800

THRIVING FAMILY®	**FOCUS ON THE FAMILY CLUBHOUSE JR.®**	**FOCUS ON THE FAMILY CLUBHOUSE®**	**FOCUS ON THE FAMILY CITIZEN®**	
Marriage & Parenting	Ages 4 to 8	Ages 8 to 12	U.S. news issues	Rev. 3/11

More Great Resources
from Focus on the Family®

Bedtime Blessings #1
by John Trent, Ph.D.
In just a few minutes each night, you can bless your child (age 7 and under) and impart spiritual truths that last a lifetime. Every bedtime activity is followed by a blessing prayer that affirms your love and deepens your child's relationship with God. Includes 100 easy-to-follow plans for read-to-me stories, amazing experiments, giggle-making games, and more.

Bedtime Blessings #2
by John Trent, Ph.D.
One hundred more terrific tuck-ins for you and your young child! Practice the biblical model of blessing—while having fun and creating great memories. Quick and simple to prepare, these "together times" include "let's pretend" activities, intriguing puzzles, blessing prayers, and more.

I'd Choose You!
by John Trent, Ph.D.
Show your children how much you (and God!) love them. When Norbert comes home from school, he's had the worst day. Picked last for the team, he feels awful. As he and his mother talk about the day's mishaps, she gently imparts the blessing to him through spoken word, meaningful touch, attachment of high value, portraying a special future, and genuine commitment.

Blessing Your Grown Children
by Debra Evans

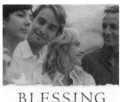

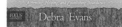

Need help with thorny issues like setting boundaries and letting go? Having trouble staying connected and trusting God when things don't turn out quite as you'd hoped? This book offers advice and encouragement every step of the way. Discover how to bless your adult children while enjoying the empty—or not-so-empty—nest.

Blessing Your Husband
by Debra Evans

Enrich your husband's life with prayer, words, and actions—and watch him come alive in your relationship. This down-to-earth guide helps you understand your spouse's thought patterns, priorities, and masculine characteristics. End-of-chapter prayers and journaling exercises equip you to practice the principles. A more satisfying marriage awaits you!

The Blessing
by John Trent, Ph.D. and Gary Smalley

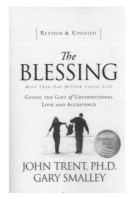

Revised and updated, this bestselling classic explains how the biblical gift of the blessing is the key to self-worth and emotional well-being. A foundational parenting tool, the blessing consists of five essential elements: meaningful touch, spoken message, attaching high value, picturing a special future, and an active commitment. Includes ideas for blessing events. And if you've missed your own parents' blessing, the final chapters are especially for you.

FOR MORE INFORMATION

 Online:
Log on to FocusOnTheFamily.com
In Canada, log on to FocusOnTheFamily.ca

 Phone:
Call toll-free: 800-A-FAMILY
In Canada, call toll-free: 800-661-9800